Silage

Bethany W. Pope

Indigo Dreams Publishing

First Edition: Silage
First published in Great Britain in 2017 by:
Indigo Dreams Publishing
24 Forest Houses
Halwill
Beaworthy
EX21 5UU

www.indigodreams.co.uk

Bethany W. Pope has asserted her right under the Copyright, Designs and Patents Act 1988 to be identified as the author of this work.

ISBN 978-1-910834-40-4

British Library Cataloguing in Publication Data. A CIP record for this book can be obtained from the British Library.

Designed and typeset in Palatino Linotype by Indigo Dreams.
Cover design by Ronnie Goodyer of Indigo Dreams.

Printed and bound in Great Britain by 4Edge Ltd.
www.4edge.co.uk

Papers used by Indigo Dreams are recyclable products made from wood grown in sustainable forests following the guidance of the Forest Stewardship Council.

For Chris Claremont, Stephen King, Piers Anthony, CS Lewis, Mike Mignola, Jean Auel, Madeleine L'Engle, and Jane Yolen. Thanks for keeping me alive.

Acknowledgements

Poems from this collection have appeared in the following magazines: *Picaroon, Rat's Ass Review, London Grip, Clear Poetry, The Open Mouse, Crack the Spine, Culture Cult, Stirred Press, Dark Horse Poetry, Winter: An Anthology for the Changing Seasons, The Journal, Well Versed,* and *More Raw Material* (Alan Sillito Anthology).

Also by Bethany W. Pope:

Poetry

A Radiance (Cultured Llama, 2012)
Crown of Thorns (Oneiros Books, 2013)
The Gospel of Flies (Writing Knights Press 2014)
Undisturbed Circles (Lapwing, 2014)
The Rag and Boneyard (Indigo Dreams Publishing 2016)

Novel

Masque (Seren, 2016)

CONTENTS

Neurons... 9
The Penalties of Bad TV 10
Killing Me Softly 11
Fallon 13
Clinton, South Carolina 14
Sweet Communion 16
Purifier.. 18
Market Day in the Children's Home 20
Autumn, 1996 21
Lesson Plan 23
Hippocampus and Amygdala.. 24
Muckraker... 25
Pecans... 26
Some Kind of Fairy Tale... 27
Uncanny X-Men 28
The World Tree 30
Carnival.. 31
Theft.. 32
Jeff Goldblum 33
Girls 35
Rows 37
Nitpicking 39
Making Hay.. 41
In My House-Mother's Office 42
Zebra Cakes 43
Cabbage.. 45
Liquid Gold 47
Sunday Morning 48
Begging Bowls... 50
Strawberry Daiquiri.. 52
Beating.. 54
Fourteen 55
The Language of Flowers.. 58
When She Asks for Bread, Will You Give Her a Stone? 59
Gemini 60

APPLICATION FOR ADMISSION

NAME OF CHILD ___Bethany Walsh Pope___

DATE OF BIRTH _____

Silage

Neurons

Our memories are physical, embossed
onto the substance of our brains. Trauma
leaves a scar that is visible, a white
thread running across your MRI. I
saw the shape of the worst years of my life
thrown up on a screen in a doctor's office;
I'd gone in to see if anything could
be done about my terrible snoring.
The scan revealed more than broken bones.
Later that year, when I'd forced my courage,
I sent off an email. My old social-
worker wrote back to tell me that most of
my records had been lost. What remained was
enough to bring back the look and scent of
wild onion-blossoms, the sharp, salt taste of
blood. I remembered what it was like to
spend days locked in the cabinet under
the stairs, surrounded by White Rain shampoo
and industrial cleaners; rags that felt like
they'd been dipped in human urine and left
to dry, stiff, across a doorknob. The thin,
white seam in my brain opened up and spilled
the rot it had been hiding. Now, I've got
to roll up my sleeves and clean it all up.

The Penalties of Bad TV

The day my father dropped me off I stole
two greasy quarters from my roommate's desk.
They were sitting, face up, in the pencil
slot and I remembered an episode
of Hey Dude which featured the mystical
Native-American character (who
was played by a Mexican) saying that coins
found face-up signified good luck for the
finder. Being twelve, and objectively messed
up, I had a loose definition of
'finding'. But then, so did every other
kid locked behind those walls. Of course, they caught
me before my father pulled his champagne-
coloured van out of the driveway. Mrs Scott,
my new social worker, ran out and slapped
her fat palms against the dented driver's-
side door so that he could witness my pockets
being roughly turned out. Twin bicentennial
quarters danced in her finger-cage. My father
sighed in that way he had which made my guts
clench with the knowledge of what was coming
and so I felt relieved that I would not
have to be alone with him any time
soon. Of course, I couldn't read the future;
how that small, impulsive theft paved the way
for greater ones when that same roommate reached
for me in the dark and tore me from the
inside out. Two quarters bought my father's
disbelief forever. Fallon found a
two-bit whore and, like most cheap prostitutes,
the profits were never really mine.

Killing Me Softly

The inmates of the younger houses ate
in the large campus cafeteria.
Older children progressively took their
meals in their cottages, learning to cook
so that, the theory went, they could function
in the world after their graduation.
By the time I reached that phase there were padlocks
on all the cabinet doors. In Brophy,
the cottage where the newest orphans were
stashed to adjust, the only in-house
food consisted of Sisco-company
off-brand rice crispy treats and nacho chips.
Sisco is a major supplier to
prisons and every morsel we ate came
either from the on-campus farm or their
warehouses. Every evening we'd gather
outside of the dark, stone-walled living-room
(the only part of the house that did not
smell like industrial cleaners — the room
the rarely-visiting parents saw) and
flock onto the back porch, into the shade
of a sprawling, spindle-limbed live-oak. Moss
flapped against the roof when the wind blew. Red
mites rained down to burrow in our naked
pores. We stood in a circle and held hands,
bowing our heads for our mandatory
prayers. One day, when it was Fallon's turn, she
squeezed my hand (my hymen-blood still drying,
dark, beneath her nails) and said, 'Dear Lord, please
help Bethany to be less stupid, less
bad.' My eyes snapped open and she smirked, 'Help

her to listen to our House-Mother and
her Student Supervisor. Lord, make her
be better. Let her be quiet and good.' I
could hear a radio playing somewhere,
at a distance; it was something I knew.
The Fugees, singing the song I was raped
to. I felt something hard and cold slide into
my guts. The world wavered, and then (praise God)
I felt nothing at all. Fallon traced her
red nail across the blue veins in my wrist.
Dinner that night was fried chicken, soggy
and cold along the pinkish bone. Dessert
was a Snickers ice-cream bar. I held it
in my lap until the vanilla warmed.
I sucked the sweet slurry heart from the milk
chocolate shell, pretending
all the time that I was pithing something else.

Fallon

You were wounded, demented, a bad little girl,
Grinning as you slid your fingers into me.
I never thought I'd catch myself praying for your soul
After you told me that, now, I could never be loved. My small
Body was a canvass for your vengeance;
You were wounded, demented, a bad little girl
Still angry at your mommy for selling you to tall,
Grown men whose cocks (you said) tasted like pee.
I never thought I'd catch myself praying for your soul
When, years later, you let your filthy orange urine fall
Into my mouth as you used your woven belt to choke me.
You were wounded, demented, a bad little girl,
And I was unsurprised when I learned you'd landed in jail,
Though the crime they nailed you for was unrelated to rape.
I never thought I'd catch myself praying for your soul,
When I spent the night vomiting after giving my all
Attempting to make love to the man that I love, but this is true:
You were wounded, demented, a sad little girl
And I just caught myself praying for your soul.

Clinton, South Carolina

They gathered us into three battered white
vans and waited while we shifted in those
gray, worn-shiny seats, buckling our belts.
I leaned against the window, attempting
sleep while the rough road vibrated my brain.
The restaurant had been cleared for the morning
(orphans get to eat before the mid-day
rush) so we were not allowed to forget
that this was just another tool to dress
us up as human. Inside there were bare
beams, kitsch, a selection of worn saddles
mounted on the walls. We had hamburgers,
identically cooked, and mugs of warm milk.
Our houseparents ordered whatever they
wished. We ate in the required silence,
filling the long room with the high echoes
of knives on cheap china and ill-timed burps.
After our meal, three waitresses appeared
with trays of bright-painted, wooden lapel
pins. We each could take one. I chose a red
parrot because they can talk, and I was
famished for words. I slipped it into my
pocket and fondled the finish all the
way back to the home. This was my first week.
I was still allowed to make (supervised)
phone calls. Red was still a colour of hope,
and meals were guaranteed at regular
intervals. I don't know where that pin went.
Maybe I lost it in one of my moves.
Maybe it was in the box of letters
Fallon pissed on when I started fighting

her fingers in the dark. I remember
the taste of that hamburger; cheap, scorched meat,
a dried-out bun; French fries the texture of
wet plaster; the waitresses wide, frightened
eyes — as though what we had was contagious.
As though we deserved to be so alone.

Sweet Communion

One of my father's seminary friends
was the chaplain for the orphanage. He
invited me to his house, once, when I
first arrived. His wife (a woman, small, in
every sense) was pregnant with their first child.
They showed me the baby's room, painted in
neutral colours, the walls already lined
with cases full of bright-bound children's books.
They left me alone with that treasure while
they went to check the roast. Saliva surged
in my throat at the sight of so much plenty.
They had the entire run of Goosebumps,
those thin slivers of horror designed to
keep children awake at night, terrified
of alien eggs, ventriloquist dummies,
and fortune-telling cameras who promised death.
We were not allowed to read this kind of
novel at home, but I was drawn to this
type of fear. It was so much nicer, more
manageable, to shoot a werewolf with
a silver slug than it was to worry
about whether your mother would die this week,
or when the next fight would happen. The kind
of fear promised in those pulpy pages
offered sweat and catharsis. I knew that,
if I asked, the good reverend would lend me
a couple of copies. But I also
feared what would happen if he told my Dad
what kind of stories they were. I did not
yet know the nature of the ground I stood on.
I did not know that I needed allies,

no matter how kind or ineffectual.
I slid four novels into the slashed, pink
lining of my jacket and read them all
that night, swallowing them down in one draught.
The chaplain saw the gaps, of course. He called
my social worker who flipped my room
and found them in the middle drawer of my desk.
There were consequences. A week later,
my father sent me a letter, written
on the back of a postcard he made from
one page of a joke-a-day The Far-Side
calendar. He told me how deeply I had
humiliated him in front of his
colleagues, how I was well on my way to
making nothing of my life, becoming
nothing, as though the heart of my self was
naturally absence. He never wrote again.
He left me there, for years, to slowly drown.

Purifier

For the first six weeks, I attended school —
though rape quickly caused my grades to slip. I
spent science class distracted by the sight
of the pair of human foetuses, stuck
fast in Lucite, that the teacher kept as
bookends. In math, I was seated beside
the girl who made my night-life hell; fractions
had no hope of holding my interest. I'd
been banned from the library already
(though Mrs. C had a habit of slipping me
books) and the taunting I endured in gym
made the idea of sports unpalatable.
It's difficult to be a team player
when the girls you face on the basketball
court have a habit of cornering you
in the locker room and rubbing fresh shit
into your face. All this stress added up.
Right before I stopped trying, resigning
myself to a state of permanent janitorial
detention, the coach announced The Presidential
Fitness Test. This was a contest composed
of pull-ups, long-jump, and sit-ups. I was
small (and getting smaller) but, by God,
I was strong. And, boy, did I ever want
to beat all of them. Skeleton light, I
hauled myself up over the bar, reed-thin,
I flew across the sand pit. When the coach
held my feet and started counting, I leapt
up over and over again until
he lost his voice entirely and his
blond hair was matted brown with sweat. After,

I walked back to the barracks feeling clean
and empty, remembering his white, innocent
grin. Almost to the door (which held nightmares
behind it) a car pulled up to the curb
and honked its duck-like horn. It was the coach.
He rolled down his window and called to me,
holding out his huge fist. When I approached,
he said, 'You did good today, kid' and dropped
five sweaty M&M's into my palm.
Grateful, a little disgusted, I took
them into my mouth, savouring sweetness, and salt.

Day in the Children's Home

There was a room full of donated clothes
sticking out from the Admin Building's gray
stone sides. It resembled a garden shed;
cheap vinyl siding and a rickety
plywood door pointing to the parking lot.
Local Presbyterian churches sent
black plastic garbage bags full of worn shirts,
high-waisted, stone-washed jeans, and disjointed toys
which were sorted into piles according to kind.
We called what we did there shopping, as though
we had a choice beyond approximate fit,
as though we were not picturing the groins,
the breasts, the lives of the bodies who filled
these forms before us, breaking them down.

Autumn, 1996

Six weeks into my interminable stay
in the orphanage, I snuck out, shrugging
my thinning shoulders into a worn-out
pink jacket. I walked fast, with my head down,
through the lovely, brown-and-gold avenue
ducking when I passed the window my house-
mother glared through when her soaps were off air.
In theory, I could contact my social-
worker whenever I wished. In practice
it was harder. The surest way involved
picking a fight with someone much bigger,
but I'd already been cut, once, across the ribs
(the shiv-blade scraped a rivet in my bones)
and the chances were good that I'd just be drugged
and thrown into the Quiet Room. I'd spent
too long sitting on that gym-mat mattress,
staring into the grilled drain on the floor
for that option to appeal to me. Wind
bit my ears as I fled across the yard.
Entering the stone administration
building, I slipped past the Secretary
(a large woman, wearing a false gray bun)
and stalked into Mrs Scott's office. Her back
was towards me. She was on the phone. When she
finally turned around she found me sitting
square in the plastic blue chair across from
her oak-veneered desk. I'd threaded my legs
through the legs of my seat (my sneakers squeaked
against those metal bars) and, seeing this,
she smiled at me with the same false sweetness
she gave my father when he signed over

custody of me to the state. 'Well now,'
she asked, 'what can I do for you?' I told
her everything. I talked about the rapes,
the beatings, how Fallon came in while I
was showering. She nodded, her mouth in
a line. She told me she'd get back to me.
I was given seventy-two hours of
extra work detail for sneaking out. I
spent the time raking leaves and mucking out
cow stalls, singing excerpts from The Beach Boys.
At the end of my sentence, she summoned me.
I sat in that same chair, watching the slow
creep of the second-hand circling around
the face of her school-room style clock. She held
me in silence for a full five minutes.
Then, she began to lie. 'I called your father
and passed on your message. He doesn't believe
you, and neither do I. We've decided
on a fitting punishment: hay-rake detail,
for the next three weeks.' Then she dismissed me.
I thought I had failed. My hands faded, numb.
But then, that night, I was taken to the
on-campus doctor. I was given a
blood test and some strong penicillin.
The next day, I was issued a red wheelbarrow and ordered to pack my black trunk.
She moved me to another house, across
the trap they called a campus. I still had
to struggle through the baling, but at least
I could sleep through the long nights alone.

Lesson Plan

I learned a lot from stolen books. Jean Auel
taught me how to make a sling for hunting.
Since I didn't have access to mammoth-
hide, I improvised with the donated,
half-rotten sleeve of a leather jacket.
Monica Hughes' Invitation to the Game
revealed that nearly every type of
grass bears an edible seed, accessed
by rolling the heads in your hands. Brian Jacques,
in his books where talking mice inhabit
their own miniature, red-walled Abbey,
revealed that the common cattail can be
fed upon from root to pollen. Its dust,
golden and sweet, becomes flour when mixed
with clear river water. This is how I
ate: I foraged, I scraped. I stole milk from
the warm teats of cows and pale strawberries
from the patches by the locked front gates. Food
was a constant, flushed preoccupation.
Another was safety. I watched a girl
hold the bright flame of a lighter against
the hard, clear pink of a toothbrush handle
until it clouded and softened enough
to accept a double-edged blade. I watched
her flick that new-made shiv through the dark cheek
of a boy who ordered her to suck his
dick. Eventually, I made one myself.
I learned to recognize the signs of birth
in cattle, gauging the spread of the cervix
by eye, learning the feel of a startled,
wet head, gripped through a membrane of tough, white
caul. Here is the lesson I took from that
place: life is persistent; it forces its way.

Hippocampus and Amygdala

The water of Lethe is clear and sweet —
You don't need to remember the barn, or the closet.
A draught of the past will reduce you to meat,
Pounded blood-and-bone, steaming on hay. Treat
Trash like trash. Sweep it away. Don't let it set.
The water of Lethe is clear and sweet —
It comes bottled in an orgasm; great,
Shuddering relief, followed by sleep. Pet,
A draught of the past will reduce you to meat.
Avoid things you once liked — a cow's sour-sweet
Breath, the liquor-stench of silage. Forget it.
The water of Lethe is clear and sweet,
And it comes with a price. A terrible heat
Spreads out from the almond and seahorse. Regret's
A draught of the past. It will reduce you to meat.
Grown-up little-girl, what on earth do you want?
Paradoxical erasure, your life; incomplete?
The water of Lethe is clear and sweet;
A draught of the past will reduce you to meat.

Muckraker

In February the water-troughs grew
thick gray rinds, ice that looked like frozen
foam you could break with a blow from the haft
of a mucking-out shovel. The milk-cows,
Guernseys and Jerseys, drank, swirling pale spit
with brown rust-water. Their muzzles trailed strands
of thick, pearly white that looked beautiful
if you could divorce them from their context.
Divorced from the context of the orphanage,
this farm was as beautiful as the cows
who pressed their huge flanks against my body,
forgetting (or unaware) that I was
small and very human. They had the eyes
of post-coital women; wide and so black
you could see your secret thoughts rising up
through those pools. You could scry your own future.
Standing there, hungry, stroking their coarse flanks,
my jaw swollen, fractured beneath livid
skin, I thought that all I saw was just one
more fantasy: a warm bed, piles of books,
a naked, broad-shouldered man I wasn't
afraid of. A man who'd never worked on
a farm, or stuck his thing where it wasn't
wanted. I drew back, sharp, when a young milker
leaned forward to nuzzle me. At this point
tenderness could only bring forth pain. I
slipped in three inches of part-frozen shit.
The sharp scent rose when I fractured the crust.
I braced myself with the blade of the scoop.
After a while, I went back to shovelling.

Pecans

A tall, dark trunk; bark with cracks like canyons
flowing with rain-water and tannin; bitter
sap. There is a clear spot beneath the boughs
where the soil is too acid for grass. Husks
litter the sand; black-green flesh-pods that feel
like labia, engorged after sex. They
feel like the lips she forced me to suck. I
have pushed that memory away from me.
I think that I am only thinking of
food, of how hungry I am. I am so
hungry. Most of these nuts are still unripe.
A hard wind blew them down over night. Their
shells are papery, the flesh inside is
shrunken and sweet; they'll make me sick if I
eat too many. I leave them for the squirrels.
The flesh-husks that have split into quarters,
revealing the tips of the shells (like black
lipsticks) hold meat that is succulent, good.
I peel the nuts free, staining my fingers
with black juice that darkens like ink; a stain
that will seem to take forever to wear
off. I crush two shells together in one
fist. They make a lovely sound; like breaking skulls.

Some Kind of Fairy Tale

In front of the cottage, there stood two trees. A door
sat, centred in a gray stone face. I stared at it from my nest
among their roots. I leapt, trembling with fear,
when my housemother called from inside. Her voice was sour
and I knew the oaks could not protect me from her tempest.
In front of the cottage stood two trees — my door
into another world. After school, after chores,
I fled to the front yard and concentrated until, at last,
light gaped among their roots. I leapt through, trembling with fear,
into the world I made from snatches of books — fire-
gods, superheroes, a mouse with a sword; ready to save me from
my past.
In front of the cottage there stood two trees. A door,
which no one else could see, swung open to cover
the memory of blood and nights spent, naked, locked in a closet.
I gaped, among those roots, trembling with fear
of discovery, unable to quit. I pictured a tower
swaying, toppling, and her trapped in a top room, falling into
the waste.
In front of the cottage there stood two trees. A door
gaped among their roots. I leapt through, trembling with fear.

Uncanny X-Men

You always remember your first. I was
working for the Physical Plant, one more
orphan kid making money for the farm.
Locals brought us their trash to sort. Sluicing
through a stack of torn or bent covers (bright
colours, firm bodies I wanted to touch)
I came across something ancient and strange.
The date in the corner was from before
I was born. The story was incredible,
some kind of superhero soap-opera:
a metal man broke the heart of a girl
and his drinking buddies (a blue demon
and a scary, hairy little man with
claws) took him out to get him drunk, beat him
silly, and teach him a lesson about
true love. At one point, the bar collapsed while
two giants fought over a spilled beer and
a dark, lovely woman sucked a man's life out
through his willing lips. I was thirteen.
I'd spent the last five hours sorting paper
into piles to be sold for pulp. My chest
was finally scabbing over from my last
knife-fight and my throat was always raw from
too many cigarettes. I thought I'd seen
everything, but here was a world where the
dead could rise, where the small could sprout sharp claws
from the backs of their hands and fight forever,
without tiring. Here, a demon could fence
like Errol Flynn, and be good, and have friends.
I needed that: stupid hope I thought I'd
outgrown. I took the comic, folded it

small, and wedged it into my underwear
before the Foreman could see what I'd done
and write me up for stealing resources.
Back in the cottage, locked into my closet,
I peeled it from my thin, sweat-moist haunches.
By the time the pages dried, I'd read it
ten times. That night, I grew another life.

The World Tree

My favourite tree was the hemlock that stood
in front of Siliman Cottage. I loved
how easily its branches peeled, like boiled
bones, and its sharp coniferous smell. I
could climb to the perilously swaying
top, fifteen feet from the loam, in under
thirty seconds. I wove myself a nest
up there, binding branches in Celtic knots.
I wore it's tiny, lizard-scale pinecones
in a necklace around my scrawny neck,
pretending they were talismans which could
open a door into another world
where talking mice did battle with weasels
and superheroes soared through the sky, or
teleported away from danger in
flashes of violet light. Up there, escape
was possible, even easy, swaying
safe in the arms of a mother I could trust.

Carnival

Standing there, stripped skeletal, I shivered with cold
in the early spring-light filtering through the windows.
Though still a child, I felt incredibly old;
hands folded across my chest-bones, my groin, like Eve after God
caught her in the garden with berry-stained lips. I froze,
standing there — stripped. Skeletal, I shivered with cold
while my housemother led the other girls around
me in a circle, chanting my sins. They'd taken my clothes.
Though still a child, I felt incredibly old.
They called me 'dogface', 'fishbreath', 'lesbian whore'. Bold
girls, all of them, grabbing the wound they punished me for.
On show,
standing there (stripped skeletal) I shivered with cold,
waiting, blank-faced, for them to get bored,
sick of explaining that rape wasn't something I chose.
Though still a child, I felt incredibly old,
as though their hands, their eyes, their spit (cold
on my cheeks) had mummified me from my hair to my toes.
I stood there, stripped skeletal, shivering with cold;
though still a child I felt incredibly old.

Theft

Picking a simple tumbler-lock is an
easy matter, requiring two long, thin
(relatively inflexible) metal
wires, a steady hand, and patience. That last
was the most difficult item for me
to find. Anxious at the prospect of capture,
I was tempted to force the gentle turning,
but some desires always overwhelm fear.
Behind this last locked door, the library
waited. I was hungry for books. Escape
never presented itself in any
other form. Novels taught me how to do
this, how to half listen, half feel for the right
kind of snap. Ian Fleming was right when
he said that you could feel it in your skull.
Entering the school was easy. I had
janitorial duties. Everyone
else, all the non-orphans, were at assembly
fondling their academic awards.
I heard their laughter and applause. My scalp
sprouted sweat-pricks. My long fingers went numb.
I heard the crack of a breaking tooth, then
the doorknob turned and I was in among
the stacks. Long ago, I'd slit the lining
of my faded neon jacket. The fake
silk sighed as threads parted before the knife.
I filled the jacket up with books. The coat
was too big for me. I didn't look too
lumpy. Besides, sci-fi novels form good
armour; broomsticks, fists, bounce right off. At night,
I'd curl up in the crack between my bed
and the wall, reading with a borrowed torch.

Jeff Goldblum

When I saw him in that open black shirt,
gleamingly oiled, and (vitally) injured
in Jurassic Park, I was ten years old.
I felt a small flutter in my stomach.
I did not understand. I caught The Fly
on Turner Classic Movies when I was
eleven. It was three in the morning
and I was awake, dreading our family
game of get-ready-for-school because it
involved so much explosive shouting. I
stopped fencing my shadow with a plastic
sword and sat still before the image of
a brilliant (beautiful) man fast growing
inhuman and mad. No one does love like
David Cronenberg. I understood why
Geena Davis stuck around long enough
to watch his ears drop off like rotten fruit.
One night, long after I figured out how
to tickle the tumblers of my bedroom
door lock with a modified paper clip,
I risked the rumoured fury of the cottage
ghost (who had a taste for girl-flesh) and snuck
down-stairs to sit in front of the T.V.
which hulked in the living room. I kept the
volume almost subliminally low,
pressing my ear against its warming flank
to listen to the dialogue. I watched
Jeff Goldblum's ship crash in a hairdresser's
unlikely swimming-pool. He emerged blue,
hairy as a wookie, but there was warm flesh
underneath. I was deeply in love until

Geena Davis brought him into her bed
and had that nightmare about four-breasted
women and sharp-toothed alien babies.
Bad things happen when you sleep with Geena
Davies. It took me much longer than you'd
think to unravel the bright thread of my
attraction; handsome, brilliant, charming, lost,
alien, injured. Often, our first loves
are aspirational mirrors. I felt
all the negatives. I needed the rest.

Girls

Sometimes, to get out of work, we'd fist-fight.
We were as close as it was possible
to be in such a place. She had a crush
on a boy with bad skin and a huge nose,
bad enough that she went red every time
he stood within ten feet of her, and she
trusted me enough to tell me what she'd
like to do with him if they were ever
alone. In return, I let her know where
I hid my stash of stolen books. Sometimes
we'd sneak into the high school to rob the
vending machines. I had a long, skinny
arm and she was good at peering around
corners. I'd aim to grab a few packets
of chocolate candies, shaped like peanuts, with
creamy peanut butter inside. We'd suck
their guts out, one at a time, sitting under
the dusty bleachers where normal kids sat
to watch graduations and plays. When we
fought, we held nothing back. We were really
fighting. I cracked her teeth; she blacked my eyes,
we tore each other bloody. This was love,
of a kind. This was deep intimacy.
We trusted each other to not go too
far. When the monotony of farm work,
those familiar dangers, grew too boring
to block out the things we were afraid of,
we'd glance at each other over a bale
of hay or a row of cabbages and nod,
once. Then we'd begin. When we fought, she wore
the face of my rapist. I don't know who

I was, for her. Someone who'd hurt her bad.
Eventually, the Foreman would bust through
the circle of kids who gathered around,
placing their bets (a coke, on the skinny
one) and pry us apart. He'd shout for a
while, then send us away to cool off in
the shit-scented milking hall. This was what
we wanted. Cool air. A little quiet.
A place to settle down and have a talk.

Rows

Before my House-Mother ordered me shorn,
I spent time every week as a practice
head for an older girl whose dearest dream
revolved around attending beauty school.
Each braid-day she'd seat me high on the three-legged
stool she stole from the kitchen and part my
lank white-girl hair into finger-friendly rows.
My hair wasn't the right texture — no style
she chose lasted longer than a day — but
I was available. So she made-do.
I didn't mind it. She was so gentle,
and I was hungry for any humane
touch. I'd close my eyes and let her work. She'd
sing Gospel songs, under her breath, and I'd
pretend that she was singing just for me.
Really, I might not have been there. I was
a means to an end, and an imperfect
one at that. I was a very bad fake
head. I was, apparently, very bad
at everything that was required of me.
The orphanage was just as racially
divided as the rest of the state. My hair
didn't sit well with anyone. It was
just one more reason to keep a good grip
on the shiv I'd made out of a toothbrush.
By the time of my shearing, I was as
relieved as I was humiliated.
That afternoon she sat on the plastic-
covered pastel sofa and positioned
me on the floor with my shoulders between
her high knees. She ran a narrow nit-comb

through the strands I was about to lose.
I still don't know why she bothered doing that,
why she comforted the doomed, but suddenly
I loved her. I loved her even as she
hummed those clippers close against my raw scalp
and threw me into the nil-space between genders.

Nitpicking

The first louse I ever saw was crawling
through the pages of a Xanth novel,
the one about the colour of a young
girl's magical panties. It was an odd
story, and a very strange bug. A long,
tube-like thorax (translucent, but threaded
with blood) attached to a head that was all
pincers. I had no idea what it was,
and I was tempted to squash it, but I'd
spent the night before in a barn, watching
pigs bleed out from new mouths that gaped, bright red
in the white fat of their necks. It was my
job to hold a steaming bucket under
that throbbing salt jet. I counted the pause
between gouts as those huge hearts stuttered out.
Remembering this, I leaned close to the page
and blew the bug to the floor of the closet
that was called my bedroom. There was a foot
and a half between the edge of my bed
and the windowless wall. I was locked in
to prevent another escape attempt.
The louse never got out either but, I
suppose, context is everything. My hell
was her paradise on earth, a land of
rude plenty. Within two weeks my scalp swarmed
with an army whose knife-like mandibles slashed
a myriad of mouths in the pale flesh of
my scalp. When my House-Mother found out
she ordered one of the older girls to
slash and burn the bloody field of combat
with clippers and a harsh chemical wash.

Shorn, I remembered my attempt at mercy.
I'd been called ugly before, many times.
This wasn't anything new. I couldn't
regret it. I was glad that my louse died
happy; I craved such an ending myself.

Making Hay

Sometimes birds got caught up by the baler.
Those sharp, hooked teeth drew them into the chute
and crushed them. My numbed hands would brush their wings
and their blood would seep into my rope-burns.
I tried not to think about it. After
my shift, I'd lave brown water from the pump
and soap myself up to my thin forearms,
and I tried not to think about stopped songs
or yellow beaks snapped in two, revealing
flat and pale tongues. Distraction was deadly;
I knew a girl my age who daydreamed — like
I did — but her timing was wrong. Her shoe
got caught in a trailing chain. She was pulled
under the flatbed truck we piled the bales
on. Her ankle bone gleamed white through the red
lips of the wound. After a while, she lost
the foot. I tried not to think about her
screaming, how it sounded like mangled song.

In My House-Mother's Office

Once a month I'd lie flat on my stomach
(cigarette ashes and polyester
carpet fibres blackening my hip bones)
and write thank-you notes to the church members
who donated my allowance. She said,
'They sent you fifteen dollars this month. Tell
them you spent half on a CD and gave
the rest as your tithe to our on-campus
church.' The carton near her hand was empty.
She plucked another from the pile and shook
free a pack of unfiltered Marlboros,
lighting one from the hot butt in her fat,
red hand. 'Sweet talk them. You're good at big words.
Maybe next month they'll send more. The taxes
are so high on these things I need every cent.'
I lied pretty well to those church women.
It was easy. All I had to do was
pretend that I had enough energy
to want more than escape. Besides, having grown
up in churches, I knew what kind of story
my audience preferred; grateful, and sweet.
On TV, the fickle Wheel of Fortune turned.
It was a pleasure to mask my life in words.

Zebra Cakes

There were ways of getting money without
my House-Mother's knowledge. The easiest
centred on the transport of illicit
goods; double-sided razor blades, stolen
from the (banned to me) art room; wrapped condoms,
brought in to school by Townie children, sold
at a high mark-up; ecstasy, weed, and
(just once) tabs of LSD printed on
Foghorn Leghorn stamps, wrapped in thick plastic.
Fallon's boyfriend arranged it. I hadn't
lived with her for a year, but her threats still
held weight. I smuggled these things from client
to client in the hot fold of my panties.
I carried a shiv, made from a toothbrush,
in the ravelled hot-pink sleeve of my jacket,
below the hidden pocket I sliced in
the lining to sneak home my books. I was
paid twice for these services; a quarter
a trip and an evenings' freedom. The coin
was enough to buy my passage
into the elementary school after
my afternoon of farm work. By the front
desk (guarded by an elderly woman
who favoured dried-blood dresses) there was a
rack of Little Debby Snack Cakes. Each
afternoon, dizzy with hunger, I'd slink
into the foyer and slide my greasy
coin across her broad, boat-like desk. She'd smile,
make a joke about how lucky I was
to eat such garbage every day and not
gain weight. I chose the same thing every time

(even then I associated routine
with good luck), carefully cradling a black-
and-white Zebra Cake in the centre of
my dirt-grimed palm. It settled right across
my long and muddy riverbank life line.
Outside, I would settle my sharp buttocks
onto the high cement curb and, very
carefully, peel the icing away from
the yellow, flesh-like sponge. Eaten in strips,
it lasted longer. Then, I'd pry the cake
into its component parts and tongue
the chemical cream from between the layers.
Finally, grunting, I'd taste the sponge. It took half
an hour to eat that cake. My brain tingled
with unsatisfied pleasure. My blood wheeled,
stimulated by the world's oldest drug.

Cabbage

We dedicated our time equally
to sustenance farming (feeding cattle,
harvesting hay, transforming calves
into veal for the finer tables in
Charleston) and decorating the campus
in a way that appealed to church sponsors.
We dug flower beds until our nails tore,
gouged our legs pruning the rose bushes,
and spent many long afternoons prying
last-season's blossoms free from the earth.
Often, they hadn't been there long enough
for their root-balls to uncurl from the shape
of the thin plastic pots the farm-boss bought
from Sam's by the pallet. We ringed those stone
cottages with capes of flowers, clothing
corpses in bridal finery. I don't
know why I stole the cabbage. I don't know
why those crinkled green and purple leaves were
on the roster in the first place. We tore
out row after row of indigo pansies
whose velvety petals were just starting to wilt,
tossing those bruised, crisp stems into bright piles,
and settling round stalks of flowering kale
into the same cavities. The urge struck
to slide one, softly, into my pocket.
I was trying very hard to forget
the image of the broken quail nest; eggs,
split and bright with blood and twitching tissues,
the grinning face of the blond boy I'd had
a crush on until that very minute
grinding the wailing mother-bird beneath

his brown, third-hand boots while I shrieked for him
to stop, please, stop. I planted the cabbage
in the bottom half of a can of Surge
and kept it hidden inside of the closet
that they called my bedroom. Who knows? Maybe
the residual caffeine spurred it to
growth. Certainly, it did grow, strange and tall.
Both the green and purple faded, like a
healing bruise, until the long, straggled leaves
were white as bleached bones. Altered, that plant lasted
years longer than its fellows. Survival
always takes its payment from your nature.

Liquid Gold

Saturdays were more laid-back. Just three hours
of chores in the morning and another two
after noon, then I could run off to the
Multiple Activities Centre to
play foosball or beg a better-liked kid
(the recipient of both regular
meals and a fat, donated allowance)
to buy me a Snickers or sugary
Coke. If I had no luck there, I would hustle
to the field at the far end of campus
where they kept the weather-warped scenery
for the annual Nativity Play
the orphanage put on to please their rich
sponsors. I liked it out there; just the cows,
myself, and the odd, disturbed mouse.
Sometimes, when I was particularly
hungry, I'd lure a fat-dugged mother over
and milk her teat straight into my cracked palm.
I'd lap that gold-white fluid with my tongue,
feeling my brain sparkle with the sudden
fuel. In the mornings, while I was scrubbing
every toilet in a three-block radius,
or hooking clear tubes to a series of
badly chapped udders, I'd picture the meals
that I could find, lying there like coins on the ground.

Sunday Morning

Church was mandatory. We sat, pew-bound,
in rows on Sunday morning. After chores,
we were allowed half an hour of T.V.
If the older girls were feeling kind, I
was allowed to pick the station. I loved
The Angry Beavers, X-Men, and Ahhhh, Real
Monsters, anything whose leads revelled in
their weirdness, or wallowed in explosive
angst. Fifteen minutes before the service
started our House-Mother would line us up
for inspection (I itched, awkward in my
shorn skull and rayon dress) before sending
us out to march, like troops or ducklings, behind
her second-in-command. At over three-
hundred pounds, she rarely left the house herself.
I felt something close to freedom, walking
then, even though I knew that the slightest
infraction (imagined or real) was noted
down and would be reported after, when
I stood in the hall, stripping off my clothes while
everyone stared. I loved the smell of the air
in the autumn. I loved the camellias
blooming, pink-petalled and lemon-scented,
along the path. I associated
Sundays with a quiet sort of kindness.
Sometimes the older girls would talk to me,
or stroke my scalp. Once, an eighteen-year-old
(who was about to age out) snuck up to
my closet and laid a kitschy Dollar-
Store kite across my bed. Wolverine glared,
claws out, from a background of white plastic.

I spent the whole afternoon sending him up
into the air. The church was constructed
of white clapboard; mission-style. The windows
were unstained. The sanctuary smelled like
dust and lemon oil. Sometimes former orphans
returned there to be married. I never
understood that. The chaplain my father
knew stood in front of the altar and preached,
always, on obedience. All I learned
was hatred for Paul. While he tore the bread
and poured out a dribble of watered-down
grape juice, the other children would whisper
and nudge their neighbours in the ribs, plotting
how they'd dispose of the Host this week. The
bread was always stale, or soggy — almost
wet. They got it for free; the grocery stores
we're able to write it off as a kind
donation. Refusing this blessing was
not an option. Those who were caught were made
to spend their free hours scrubbing out cow stalls.
Most of the girls I knew would press the pulpy
body of Our Lord into the moist pocket
between their lips and gums. During the last
prayer, they'd spit Christ into their hands and add
Him to the layer of spit and bread that grew
and hardened beneath the lips of the pews.
I never did this myself. I needed
all the help that I could get. Every week,
I swallowed Him like a penance. I prayed
that this rank Communion would be the last.

Begging Bowls

So much of it was asking for money.
On Sundays, when our workload was light,
we'd spend the afternoon stuffing brochures
into envelopes. The admin office
would deliver boxes of these begging-
letters; slick-printed, loaded with pictures
of smiling children (clean, in new-looking
clothes) playing on swings or standing in groups
with their arms locked around their neighbours' waists.
They were never anyone I'd ever
met, though I'd seen some of them before, in
the kind of magazines that sell mid-range
children's clothes. Everyone had a quota —
five-hundred letters a piece — even our
House-Mother, though I usually did hers.
These days weren't so bad. We'd sit on the couch,
or on the floor of the T.V room, watching
Jerry Springer's daily parade of freaks
(I will never forget the face of the
fat, bearded man who married his donkey
by placing a thin, gold band around its
delicate hoof) and the room would fill with
the whisper-shush of paper and muted,
curse-filled shouts. Everyone was focused on
getting it done as quickly as they could.
Everybody had plans. Leesha wanted
to meet up with her boyfriend, practice her
braiding on his abundant hair. Jenny
wanted to walk to the run-down local
library to research traditional
methods of abortion. Michelle needed

to finish before her MacDonald's shift
started at five so that she'd have a chance
to earn more than our House-Mother took as
her cut. I was happy with this frail peace.
As long as I was quiet, I could stay
and nobody would curse, or hit me. Their
bodies radiated a subtle heat.
It felt like a variety of love.

Strawberry Daiquiri

In the summertime, our schedules varied;
I spent eight hours a day shifting mulch from
a huge, slightly steaming pile (like a herd's
worth of triceratops droppings) onto
the orphanage's hundreds of flower
beds. Seeming was much more important than
being; the look of the place was paramount.
None of the sponsors ever glanced at our
hands. I loved the sour, fermented scent of
half-decayed cedar. I loved the fragrance
of silage; dung was an excellent base-
note for sweet Timothy hay. My rusted
red wheelbarrow had a deflated front
tyre. My shovel had a splintered handle.
I sang while I worked, hymns from church, songs from
the radio. Sometimes I was happy.
Exhaustion burns out painful emotions.
Endorphins are a free and natural
drug. After lunch, sometimes, I would be let
into the kitchen. The cabinets would,
occasionally, be unlocked. I would
heat up a can of Campbell's Vegetable
Beef Soup, or make a tuna fish sandwich,
and read the comics. I would always read
the comics, whether I had lunch or not.
At three, the second shift began. Two hours
of housework. I would clean the ten toilets
without gloves. This was my punishment
for whatever infractions I'd gathered
the day before. One of the girls in our
cottage was HIV positive. Her
fluids were used as a threat. While I cleaned,
she would lock herself into her room and
blast Tupac. Free from five to six-thirty,
I would walk off of the stone and ivy

compound, through the depressed town whose stores sold
the milk and grain we harvested. Sometimes,
I would wander into a store, purchase
a twenty-five cent cigarette from the
barrel by the door, and shoplift a comic
book. I knew my heroes would not approve,
but a girl will do anything to spend
time with her friends. At the end of the road
there was a MacDonald's. Its sign was cracked,
the yellow arches faded, pale as the
petals on a dried daffodil. The girl
from my cottage who tolerated me
best worked behind the counter. She was a vegan
chain-smoker, mad for the theatre. She lunched
on buns; empty, save for a tomato
slice. One time she bought me a dollar scratch-
off lotto ticket and, when four lemons
appeared beneath their foil circles, she used
the five dollars I won to buy me some
porn. I read that issue of Playgirl from
cover to cover while we talked about
the various penises attached to
the men who reclined in hay-piles, or lounged
by neon-blue pools. I loved the flaccid
Johnsons best. They reminded me of snail
eyes. I wanted to try to make them expand
or retract. Knowing that supper was not
an option for me, we'd stop at a white
corrugated shack that slouched at the end
of a nowhere road. She'd order herself
a banana flavoured shaved-ice from the
fat, toothless girl who spread her breasts across
the counter and spent her days dying snow.
I would always choose Strawberry Daiquiri.
Though, I'm sure, it wasn't alcoholic,
there was a thread of bitterness beneath
the sweet. I drank and felt the thrill of work.

Beating

My door was always locked from the outside,
so I pried the paint away from the frame
of the third-story window and slid down
the long copper gutter-spout, pretending
to be The Amazing Spider-Man as
I rushed towards the frozen December ground.
I wasn't wearing anything. My clothes
were taken from me when I came in from
work. I kept a huge pair of overalls
in the shed with the boiler. Slithering
into this borrowed skin, I tried not to
think about the kittens who were born here,
who I fed and kept secret until their eyes
opened and they wandered out into the yard.
I tried not to think about their bones and
bloody pelts scattered, bright, against the grass.
I tried not to picture the red teeth of
the lawn edger or the grin of the boy
who'd fallen dreamily in love with death.
Dressed, I flew for the barn where the new-made
steer were kept until the date of their slaughter.
Their door was never locked, and it was breath-
warm beneath those eaves. When I made my calls
home (under supervision) I made up
stories about making pets of these calves.
I wanted to save them and I couldn't,
except through stories. In reality,
the most I could manage was some mutual
comfort. I wandered from stall to stall, bathed
in the spoilt milk of their breath, lying down
against their soft, fattened bodies, feeling
the slow throb of their hearts through the taut drum
of my skull. Their pulses beat as slowly
as my mother's when her veins were flooded
with prescription morphine. Sometimes, I slept.

Fourteen

Six months after I stopped talking, I earned
enough good-conduct points to qualify
to spend two weeks at the local Christian
summer camp. The orphanage sent its best-
behaved children there, as a mandatory
treat; we swam in the molasses-coloured
river, rowed canoes, crafted wallets out
of scrap leather and paid for it all with our
sweat. Eight hours a day, from seven to three,
we worked in the kitchens, scoured clean the grounds,
and wore down our toothbrushes by scrubbing
the grout in the toilets reserved for the
regular campers. When we finished for
the day, we play-acted children. The paying
customers knew that we were there (they saw
us serving their meals and scraping their scraps
into the bins while they sat at their tables,
singing folk-hymns or making their complacent
prayers) but they never had to interact
with us. In the afternoons, during our
two-hours of leisure, they sat in the cool
of their air-conditioned cottages (ours,
being older, were screen-sided sheds) watching
films expounding on the nature of faith.
At night I lay in the top bunk, sweating,
above a girl who did not know my name.
My sleeping bag was meaty in texture,
and it smelled strongly of ancient urine;
it had never been washed. I drew the slick
green cloth to my neck, thinking about how
many other bodies it had held. I

listened to the wind and pressed my chapped lips
to the screen to suck the moisture that beaded
between those rusted wires. Three days before
our tenure ended, I was called into
the main lodge, where the lucky ones put on
their plays. The head counsellor was tall, blond,
with crab-apple breasts. She smiled at me
and held out a flat package. I opened
it right there in the hall. It had come from
my parents, at home in Florida. This
was the first gift I'd had from them in two
years. Apparently, it was my birthday.
I had totally forgotten. Inside,
there was a letter (filled with nice nothings)
and a professional, portrait-style picture
of my Dalmatian framed in heavy wood.
My dog was sitting, looking out at the
camera over his dichromic shoulder.
He was wearing my father's faux tortoise-
shell sunglasses. There must have been something
in my face, just then. I felt nothing save
for a strange numbness in my chest and hands,
but the counsellor knelt down beside me
and placed her huge, calloused palms on my hard,
knobbly shoulders. She touched her forehead to
mine and said, 'Honey, honey, it's going
to be OK.' I felt nothing. The world
grew dark around the edges. I clutched the
picture to my chest, and ran. I have no
memory of the next few hours. I woke,
curled up in the mud beneath an over-
turned canoe. It was dark and the mosquitoes

were biting. I had missed supper, and prayers.
The next day I had to work extra hours
on punishment detail. No one took the
photograph away. I wished that they would.
Now, after a decade and a half, it's
hanging high above my bed, in between
a print of Dürer's masochistic Saint Jerome
and Bronzino's warped 'Allegory of Love'.
I like to keep it close, but I rarely look.
It's still raw. Some memories are like that.

The Language of Flowers

My mother lied, saying yellow roses
were her favourite flower because jonquils were
out of season when she married in June
and she didn't want my father to know
that not everything about their wedding
was perfect. My father was in love with
the idea of perfection. He hated
everything that did not fit. A June-baby,
out-of-season, inappropriately
sexed, I could never be perfect. I loved
roots more than blossoms, and soil more than scent.
When I was twelve, I woke in the orphanage.
In early spring the garden-plots bled white-
and-orange daffodils, so flawlessly
formed that it hurt me to look at them. I
couldn't ever look away. Crouching down
between fleshy green stalks and the icy
stone wall of Siliman Cottage, I breathed
the scent of stem-sap, cedar, cow manure,
remembering the feel of my mother's hands,
how she'd stroke my hair when she was in pain
and we'd lie there together in the breath-
moist dark. I found out today that jonquils
and daffodils are both members of the
Narcissus family; emblems of dangerous
self-absorption. My father cares nothing
for either of them. My mother convinced
herself that yellow roses are what she
wanted all along. The bright bell-mouths of
daffodils peal echoes through the folded flesh
of my brain. I see them and remember
that cold stone wall, and the terror behind it.
I feel my nails scraping a nest of white roots.

When She Asks for Bread, Will You Give Her a Stone?

My father wrote, 'We've nothing to complain of,'
speaking of home in his infrequent letters.
'She's been treated with discipline and firm love.'
Said my social worker in her annual report. Speaking of
letters, mine home were censored to obscure the rapes.
My father wrote, 'You've nothing to complain of,
so why won't you behave? They said you shoved
a girl for no reason, that you steal and refuse your duties.
You've been treated with discipline and firm love,
and you're there until your character's reformed. You have
an opportunity. Most children in that place don't have parents,'
my father wrote, 'you've nothing to complain of.'
Meanwhile, Fallon held a knife to my throat, shoved her rough
fingers deep inside me, tongued my ear during supervised phone
calls.
'She's been treated with discipline and firm love,
according to the values of this Home', a trove
of records fell to me today, at last. On the discharge papers
my father wrote, 'We have nothing to complain of.
She's been treated with discipline and firm love.'

A few weeks before my fifteenth birthday
a friend of mine distracted everyone
by ageing-out of the dubious arms
of state custody. She took the money
she'd saved from working at McDonald's, packed
her lead-pencil drawings, Wallflowers albums,
and clothes into a green surplus duffle
and sped off in a cab to God-knows-where.
While everyone was out saying goodbye
from the verandah, I was popping the lock
on the dining room door. I plugged the phone
into the wall-socket and made my call.
Talking fast, I told my mother a cleaner
version of history, 'Yes, she beat me.
Yes, she held me down and peed into my
mouth and hair' and then I lied to save my
sanity, 'No, she just showed me hers. She
never actually touched me.' I thought that
I was marked enough without that detail.
I felt my hands grow numb as slabs of steak
laid out to age in trays of ice, hearing
her say that she believed me. My father
did not. Mom had to compromise to get
me out of there. First, she flew up for a
surprise visit, shocking my social worker.
She stayed in the cottage set aside for
court-mandated parental visitation;
a small granite hut, quaint on the outside,
all institutional linoleum
within. The air in the bedroom smelled like
damp, vomit, and fresh paint spread over blood.

The next morning I loaded her walker
into the trunk of her rental-car and she
drove us to the mall where we saw Dante's
Peak in the dollar movie theatre. On
the way to the parking lot we passed a
Christian bookstore whose windows were filled with
overblown painted calendars. One showed
a good-looking man dressed in jeans and a red
t-shirt who had crumpled backwards into
the bloody hands of Jesus. I flinched at his
despairing eyes and the way he clutched
the wooden, nail-pounding mallet. I could
not stop crying. My breath came out in snorts
and jags. Mother bought me the calendar,
along with a pair of neon-green leggings
and a flowing, floral polyester
blouse. Sliding her credit card across
the counter, she said, 'We have to hurry
now, my love.' We had an appointment
at three O'clock. My father needed proof.
The gynaecologist was very nice.
She gave me a small stuffed dog to clutch as
I laid back in the stirrups, gritting my teeth.
She did not tell me what she found. Mother
kept schtum. Whatever she uncovered down
there, my father couldn't argue with it.
I went back on antibiotics. We
returned to the cottage and ordered a large
pizza, loaded with vegetables. We ate
ice-cream from the tub with a matched set of spoons.
The next day she flew back to Florida.
Three weeks later, after my birthday, my

father finally agreed that I could come
home — though he kept back a few provisions.
I had to be good, be obedient,
I had to hold myself in and support
the myth they'd spread that I had been in boarding-
school. I had to agree to go to a
school that had been designed for children with
severe brain injuries where I spent my time
reading books I held, hidden, in my lap,
finishing the day's work in five
minutes. I held my tongue about my migraines;
I had long ago grown used to the symptoms
of prolonged fear. I had to smile, and say
that my experience had been very
good for me when Dad recommended that
other parents send their troubled children
to that stone-and-ivy Dis. I agreed.
I kept up my side of the bargain because
my packed trunk never budged from its place
by the front door. I lasted eighteen months
before sneaking to the real high-school and
taking the tests which would win me a full
scholarship and early-admittance to
University. But all of that came
after I was welcomed back to the family
with a belated birthday party.
Sitting in the restaurant, my long legs
wrapped around the metal legs of my chair,
I kept my head down while my family sang
to me. I cut the cake which bore my name.